AF393274

Soul of Lisbon

A GUIDE TO EXCEPTIONAL EXPERIENCES

AUTHORS: FANY PÉCHIODAT, LAURIANE GEPNER AND LUCIE ETCHEBERS
ILLUSTRATIONS: COLINE GIRARD
PHOTOS: PAULA FRANCO @LISBONBYLIGHT

JONGLEZ PUBLISHING

Travel guides

ATUM NATURAL
MINOR
ATUM NATURAL
MINOR

"FOR A LONG TIME,
WE KEPT THIS CODE WORD
TO OURSELVES: LISBON.

IF THINGS TOOK A BAD TURN,
THE WHITE CITY WOULD BE
OUR SAFE HAVEN."

OLIVIER FRÉBOURG

WHAT YOU WON'T FIND
IN THIS GUIDE

- the route of Tram 28
- the address of the Santa Justa elevator
- the most touristy dinner and fado show

WHAT YOU WILL FIND
IN THIS GUIDE

- the best vegetarian meal of your life
- the joy of running on clouds
- a party venue the size of a palace
- fifty shades of green in the middle of the city
- where to dine in an Ali Baba's cave

This guide is not comprehensive – and it doesn't aspire to be. There are other guides for that.

Our M.O. is the opposite of overwhelming you with options. Instead of suggesting 1,000 ideas you won't have time to explore in just a few days anyway, we've chosen just 30. Obviously, we were very tempted to stretch that to 40, or even 50 ... But we stuck to our guideline. As a result, we scoured Lisbon without counting our steps, climbed and hurtled back down hills, chatted with the characters who crossed our path, sampled every edible thing to be found in the city, drank a few nectars (guided by our professional code of ethics) and explored all the nooks and crannies, passages and alleyways ...

And here you are, holding the fruits of our labour in your hands. A selection of 30 experiences in Lisbon to savour, make your own and – we hope – love.

SYMBOLS USED IN
SOUL OF LISBON

< 10 euros

10 to 40 euros

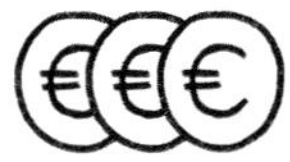

> 40 euros

First come,
first served

Reservation
recommended

100% Lisbon

Opening times often vary,
so we recommend checking them directly
on the website of the place you plan to visit.

Some call it magnetic; others compare it to an aging woman who has lost almost all her finery but still has style. Some claim it's eternal; others that it's losing its soul as the face of the city changes. Maybe the truth can be found – as is so often the case – at the intersection of history, memories and dreams, both collective and personal. Somewhere in a tram lurching across the ages and hills; in the dusky pink of a façade in Mouraria, blushing as a ray of sunlight skims it just so; in the beating heart of the city, Chiado; in the cheeky humour of Graça; or in the majesty of Belém. In the *miradouros* perched on the city's highest points. And, finally, in the Tagus River, which flows into the ocean across which the great 15th- and 16th-century Portuguese explorers set sail and returned home.

Lisbon is like the movement of these waves, flowing between the open ocean and shore. Are we in a can't-miss capital of the start-up scene, a young and creative city, forward-looking and tech-driven? Or in one of Europe's oldest cities, covered with azulejo tiles, whose thousands of blue eyes have been watching us, unblinking, for several centuries? The answer is: both. Lisbon juggles with time, jumping from past to near future across two thresholds. Here, a supremely Instagrammable coffee shop with clean lines; there, a boutique that's been around since 1789 and still makes candles the old-fashioned way – today as it did yesterday, as it will tomorrow. Or maybe not: Lisbon's fate is cause for concern. The old boutiques are closing their doors; with each façade that is renovated, a bit more of the Lisbon of yesterday disappears.

Yet there's one thing about Lisbon that isn't ready to change: the light. So unique it could give anyone the crazy idea never to leave the city again – or to leave everything else for it. A light born of the reflection of the water on the Tagus, called the "Sea of Straw" (Mar da Palha) for its golden shimmer. A light that paints the cobblestones white, splashing across everything in its way, the façades dancing along with it like shadow puppets. Lisbon is written in this eternal light, of which one Lisbon native said, "I've never seen similar light anywhere else. Grey days are my favourite: the cobblestones are of such pure white they seem to be infinite in volume." She then went on: "Lisbon is a poem to look at." We'd add: "and to discover." And here are 30 experiences to prove it.

ANTONIO
KNIFE-SHARPENER

30 EXPERIENCES

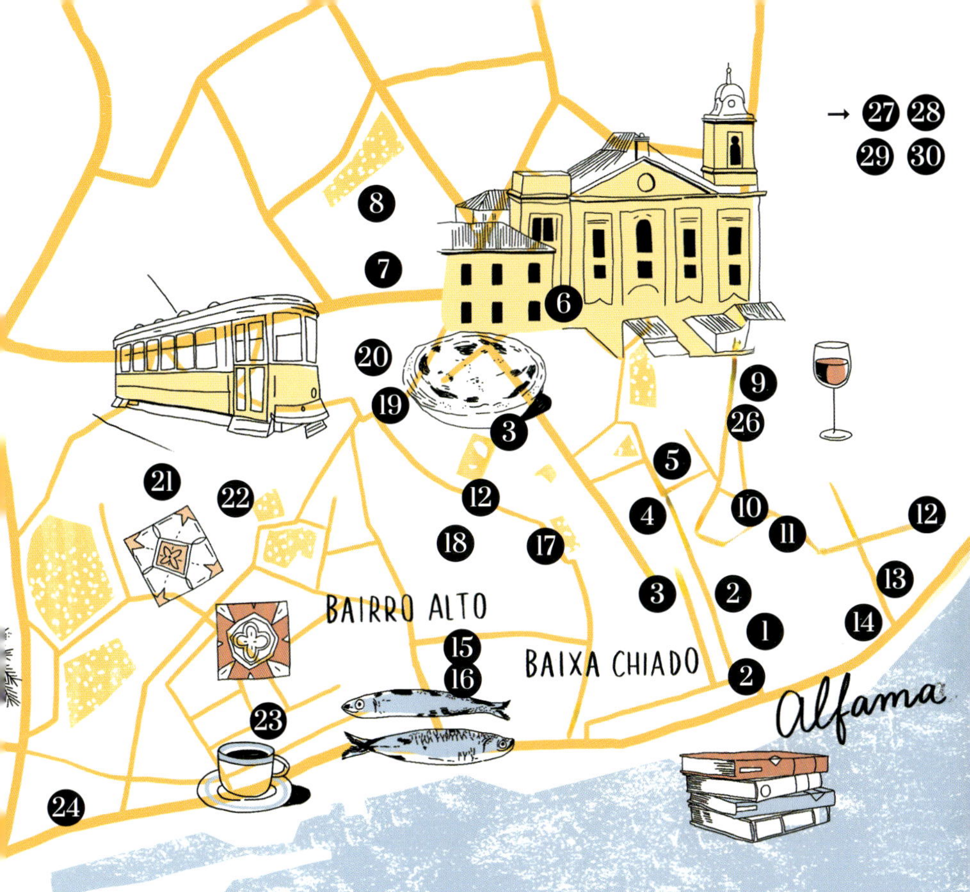

27 28
29 30
8
7
6
20
19
3
9
26
5
4
12
10
11
12
18
17
13
21
22
14
BAIRRO ALTO
3
2
1
2
BAIXA CHIADO
15
16
Alfama
23
24
Ponte
S DE ABRIL
Almada
25

PRADO
TRAVESSA DAS PEDRAS NEGRAS 2

+351 21 053 4649

pradorestaurante.com
Instagram: @prado_restaurante

THE TEMPLE OF
PORTUGUESE NOUVELLE CUISINE

Prado means 'meadow' in Portuguese. And that's where chef Antonio Galapito, aka the rising star of Portugal's food scene, takes his inspiration. After having learned the ropes with chef Nuno Mendes in London, Galapito now champions 'cuisine libre' (free cuisine) at his Lisbon restaurant, inspired by the farm-to-table movement. Ingredients that come from all across the country, dishes whose composition changes daily depending on the season and the chef's mood ... The only constant: the flavour of Portugal today.

- ANTONIO GALAPITO -

CHEF AT PRADO

What's your oldest cooking-related memory?

I was born near Sintra, where suckling pig is a specialty. Maybe even more than the taste, it's the smell of it that makes my mouth water … My mother would grill it over a wood fire, and you could smell the aroma of garlic, paprika, white wine, and black pepper.

Do you serve it at Prado?

Sometimes, but cooking it for seven to eight hours in a normal oven is a bit more technical. The way we serve it is also different from the traditional recipe: meat, sauce, and … that's it. Bye-bye, trimmings. The meat is so tender, there's no need for anything else.

When did you know you wanted to become a chef?

When I was 14, I was terrible at school. I wasn't passionate about cooking; I didn't even particularly love eating – in fact, for me, a good steak was a well-done steak, which gives you some idea … But that's when my mother suggested I go to cooking school. So I went – and never looked back.

And if you were to do something else …?

No, I don't see myself doing anything else. Or maybe a farmer, when I'm 60 years old?

Is Prado a Portuguese restaurant?

Yes, to the extent that we source all of our ingredients (except for sugar) from Portuguese food producers all across the country. That's our only rule, and we build our menu – which changes a bit every day, depending on what gets delivered and our inclinations – around it. When we see new fish, we always ask if it was caught in Portuguese waters. If not, we don't take it!

Your à-la-carte guilty pleasure?

It varies every day, but some dishes are always on the menu and don't change much. One of my favorites (maybe even my absolute favorite!) is the bread, served with a paste made of goat's-milk butter, smoked coarse salt, pork fat, garlic, and caramelised onion compote ... I can't get enough of it!

A fun fact about Portuguese cuisine?

The Portuguese have always been great travelers. Did you know that they brought tempura to Japan? And when they returned from their expeditions, they brought back yuzu, which now grows in Portugal. We use it in the Prado kitchens instead of lemon: it immediately transports you to another place.

02

SINK YOUR TEETH
INTO A *BIFANA*

A *bifana* is to the Portuguese what a ham-and-cheese sandwich is to the British: a simple, quick and inexpensive solution that rarely disappoints. It consists of a very finely sliced pork cutlet, marinated in dry white wine, lemon juice, bay leaves, paprika and garlic, and gently basted in its own juices, nestling between two slices of *papo seco* (Portuguese bread). To spice things up, spread on some mustard right before you sink your teeth into it and then wash it down with a few glasses of wine. For an even more decadent experience, bite into a *leitão*, a typical Portuguese sandwich made with suckling pig.

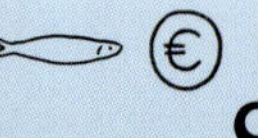

For *bifanas*:

AS BIFANAS DO AFONSO
R. DA MADALENA 146

instagram.com/explore/locations/
440586039731769/as-bifanas-do-afonso

For *leitãos*:

NOVA POMBALINA
RUA DO COMÉRCIO 2

+351 21 887 4360

TURIM
NOVA POMBALINA

SEE A FILM
UNDER THE OPEN SKIES

Around when the sun sets over the Tagus, one of the great pleasures Lisbon has to offer is watching a film in an open-air cinema.

> CINE SOCIETY

Perched on the rooftop of the Cine Society, with the city as a backdrop, settle back comfortably into a deckchair with a cocktail in hand as you prepare to (re)discover a classic film under the stars.

> LA CINEMATECA

The Cinemateca has the best film programme in Portugal, hands down. And, in summer, it also screens quality films on a delightfully secluded terrace, taking you on a real trip back in time, far from the tourist crowds. Before the screening, you can also dine alfresco and visit the Cinemateca bookshop, a paradise for film buffs.

Open-air films generally start at around 9:30pm. As a general rule, you must purchase tickets on site and cannot reserve them in advance – with one exception: if you book a table for dinner on the terrace just before an evening screening, you can also reserve tickets for the film.

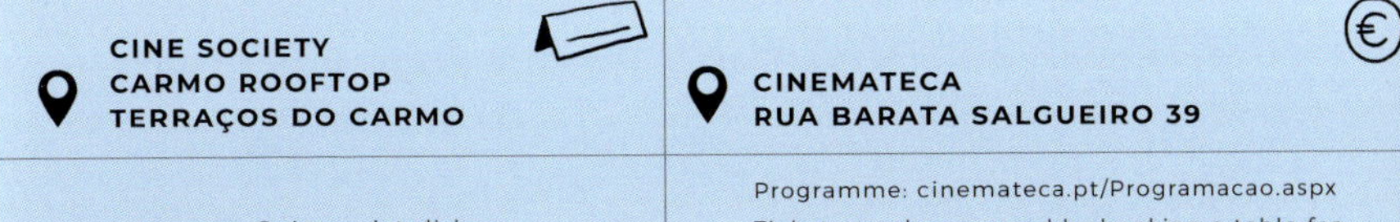

CINE SOCIETY
CARMO ROOFTOP
TERRAÇOS DO CARMO

Instagram: @cinesociety.lisbon
cinesociety.pt

CINEMATECA
RUA BARATA SALGUEIRO 39

Programme: cinemateca.pt/Programacao.aspx

Tickets can be reserved by booking a table for dinner: contact the restaurant 39 Degraus
+351 960 396 370 or + 351 911 904 075

THREE BAR STOOLS,
ONE BAR

It's a Portuguese spirit(s)ual question, but there is a world beyond port wine. And, in this world, Ginja, or Ginjinha (sour-cherry liqueur), holds centre stage. For a long time, the Ginjinha Sem Rival (Unrivalled Ginjinha) bar, which opened in 1890, made its own in the back shop. And the question customers are asked the moment they rest their elbows on the counter hasn't changed since the 19th century: 'Com o sem elas?' (With or without cherries?) We recommend with – even though (or especially because) it's dangerous! Your little glass will be served filled to the brim, as tradition dictates. As for whether or not it's truly the best Ginjinha, you'll simply have to head across the street to try out the neighbouring bar's version for yourself …

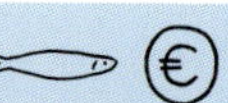

 **GINJINHA SEM RIVAL**
R. PORTAS DE SANTO ANTÃO 7

+351 21 346 8231

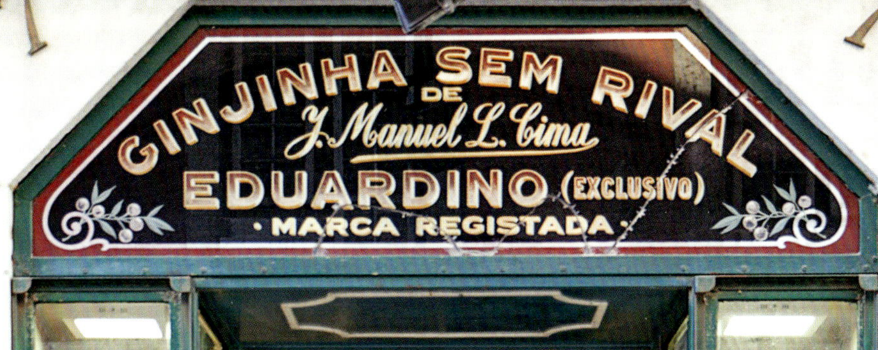

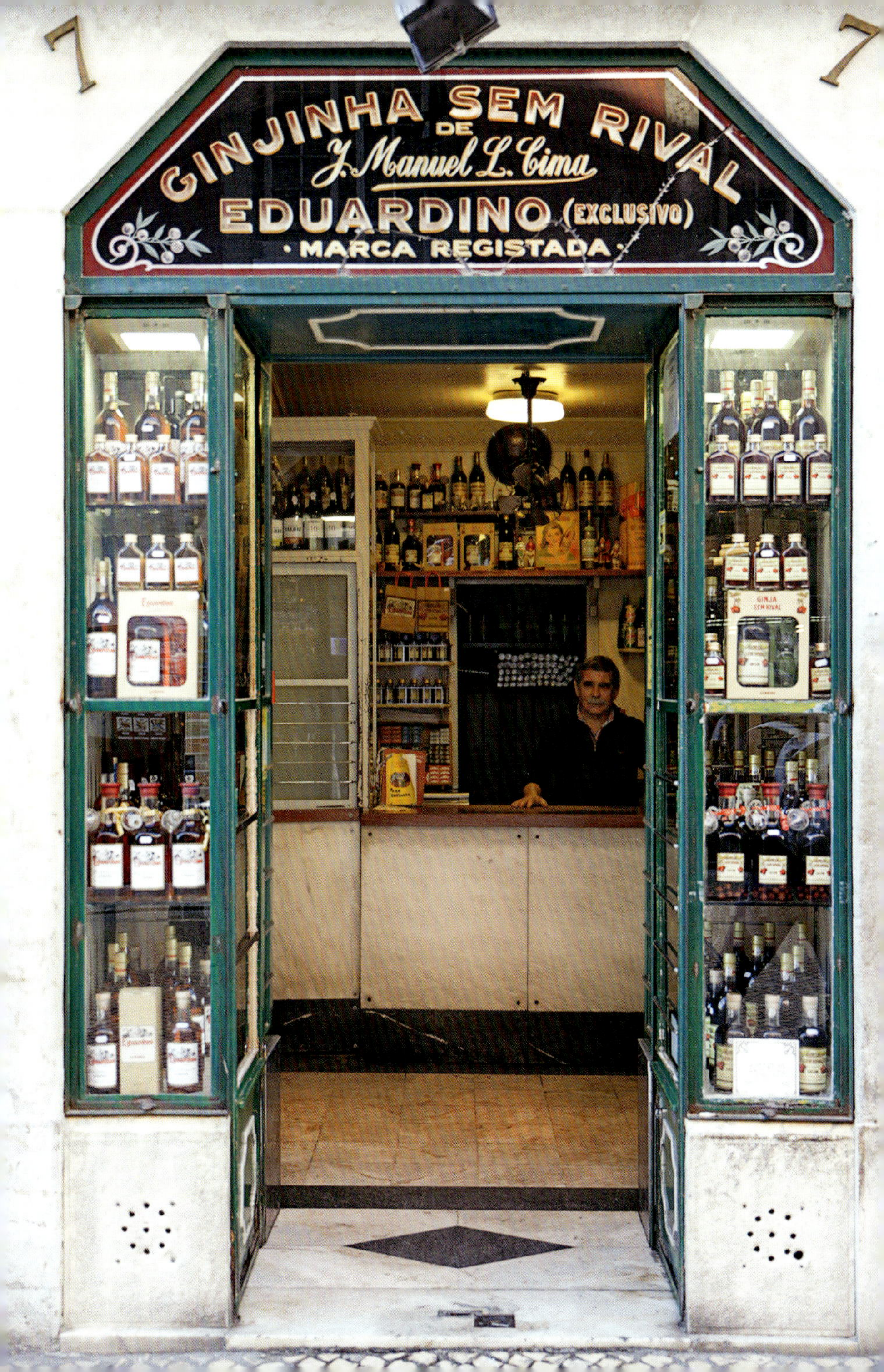
GINJINHA SEM RIVAL
DE
J. Manuel L. Cima
EDUARDINO (EXCLUSIVO)
· MARCA REGISTADA ·
GINJA
SEM RIVAL

ROOMS WITH VIEWS:
LISBON AT YOUR FEET

Put your heart-to-heart with Lisbon on hold for the night? No, thanks. Instead, choose to fall asleep with Lisbon at the foot of your bed and wake up to the same vision, daytime version. Here is a selection of rooms we recommend:

MEMMO ALFAMA

This hotel is hidden away in the Alfama district, at the end of a cul-de-sac paved with uneven cobblestones. Up on the roof terrace, slide into the red swimming pool to do a few laps with a view. And in rooms 31 and 33, the Alfama is right there at the foot of the bed, a labyrinth of rooftops unfurling all the way down to the Mar da Palha (Sea of Straw).

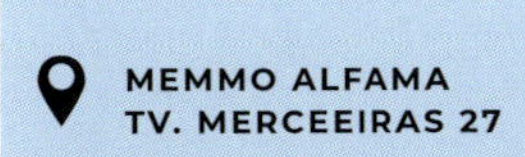

MEMMO ALFAMA
TV. MERCEEIRAS 27

+351 21 049 5660

memmohotels.com/alfama
Instagram: @memmoalfama

Torel Palace

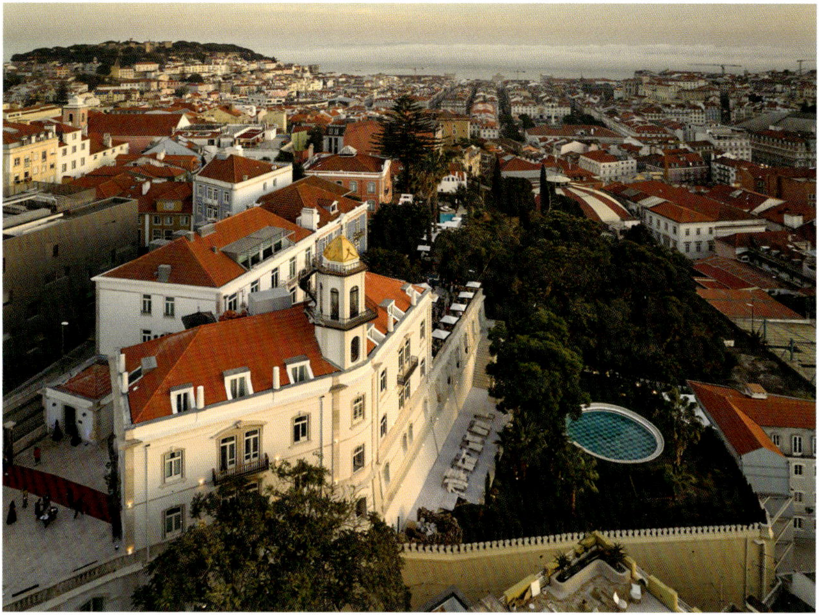

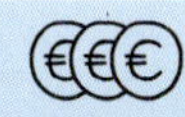

TOREL PALACE LISBON

A great location at the top of the Hill of Sant'Ana, just a few steps from the Jardim do Torel. Regardless of what room you're staying in, the terrace, swimming pool and royal peace and quiet await you. But we recommend putting your bags down in room 6, 8 or 28: big windows, small balcony and an insane view of the heart of the city.

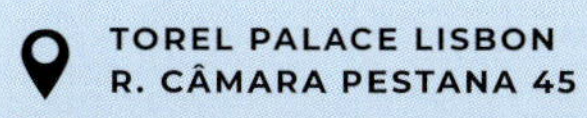

TOREL PALACE LISBON
R. CÂMARA PESTANA 45

€€€

+351 21 829 0810

torelpalacelisbon.com
Instagram: @torelpalace_lisbon

MEMMO ALFAMA
© MEMMO ALFAMA

DINE
IN A CABINET
OF CURIOSITIES

The experience at Comadre begins at the entrance, hidden behind the mirror of an old wooden cabinet. This is a secret passage to an enigmatic restaurant. Best described as an industrial Ali Baba cave with Art Deco looks.

You eat surrounded by strange objects with bouquets of dried flowers hanging from the ceiling. In what was once a cellar, you'll discover a cabinet of curiosities and two rooms decorated with heavy velvet curtains that bring to mind a David Lynch interior. Immerse yourselves in this esoteric atmosphere sipping a lavender gin sour cocktail while chilling in soft old chairs. To end the dinner, the dreaded 'fortune cookie' will deliver a message from the universe … You come out amazed, as if after a strange journey through time.

COMADRE
RUA LUCIANO CORDEIRO 81C

Instagram: @comadre_lisboa

RUNNING LAPS
ON A ROOFTOP

Enter the hotel, walk confidently towards the elevator, get in and push the '-1' button. When you reach the spa, buy a day pass. Get changed and take the elevator to the 11th floor. A vision overlooking the Tagus: a running track on the roof. So you can race against the sun and challenge the clouds, legs in the air, eyes taking in a 360°-view of Lisbon. Pure magic.*

*Since this magic is on the pricey side, this 5-star running experience is a good gift idea. A day pass includes admission to the fitness room and spa. We guarantee that you (or the recipient of your gift) won't regret it.

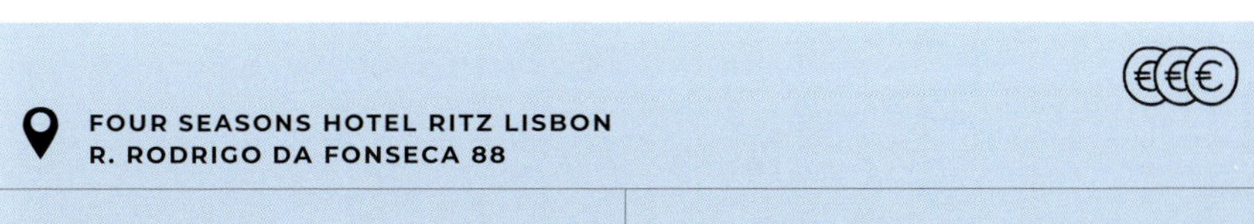

08

GO FOR A STROLL
IN THE ESTUFA FRIA

The greenhouse in the north of Eduardo VII Park is reminiscent of a Rousseau painting. Huge plants tickle the sky. Well, almost – this is a greenhouse, after all, so wooden blinds form a roof overhead ... even as they let the sunlight filter in. Come late in the afternoon, when the day is gently fading and the sky turning pink. To the left of the central alley, a small door leads to the arid and tropical greenhouse (Estufa Fria). Giant banana plants, cactuses that defy all norms ... Where in the world are we? Right in the heart of the city!

ESTUFA FRIA
PARQUE EDUARDO VII

+351 21 817 0996

estufafria.lisboa.pt

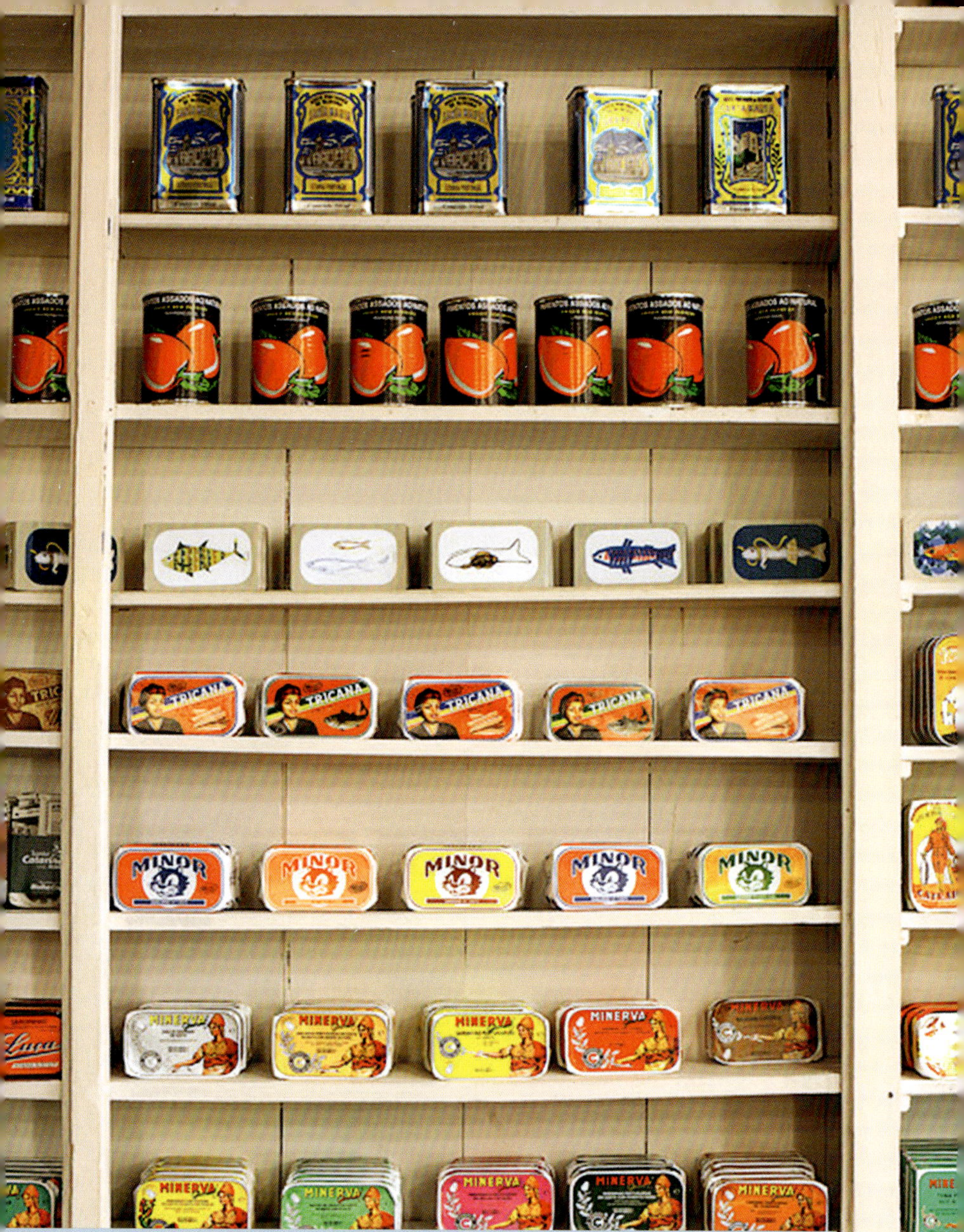

A VIDA PORTUGUESA
LARGO DO INTENDENTE PINA MANIQUE 23

+351 21 197 4512

avidaportuguesa.com
Instagram: @avidaportuguesa

#09

LISBON'S BEST
CONCEPT STORE

This is the Portuguese answer to Eataly – but not just for edibles. This concept store, the biggest of the four spaces created on the initiative of Catarina Portas, brings together the best artisanal products from all over Portugal. Its 500 square metres progress through an evolution from one room to the next. First, there's the living room, where the wool blankets will make you want to settle down for a nap; then you take a turn towards the kitchen, between ceramics and gourmet food products, before finally ogling the stationery items and ointments. Everything has been carefully selected and is beautifully presented. We double dare you to leave empty-handed.

A VIDA PORTUGUESA
© LOLA INTENDENTE

AN APERITIF
UNDER THE STARS
ON LISBON STEPS

When you've had enough of cod, head to this little restaurant in an alleyway of the old Mouraria district. Opened in 2012, this is the city's first fully vegan restaurant. In this unique venue you can simultaneously meet regulars, local residents and passing travellers seated directly on the steps transformed into terraces. On sunny days, musicians play at the foot of the steps, as in an open-air amphitheatre – perfect for a drink at the end of the day. The menu, creative and seasonal, changes regularly. Remember to book, especially in summer.

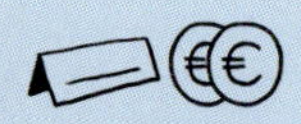

THE FOOD TEMPLE
BECO DO JASMIM 18

+351 21 887 4397

thefoodtemple.com
Instagram: @the_food_temple

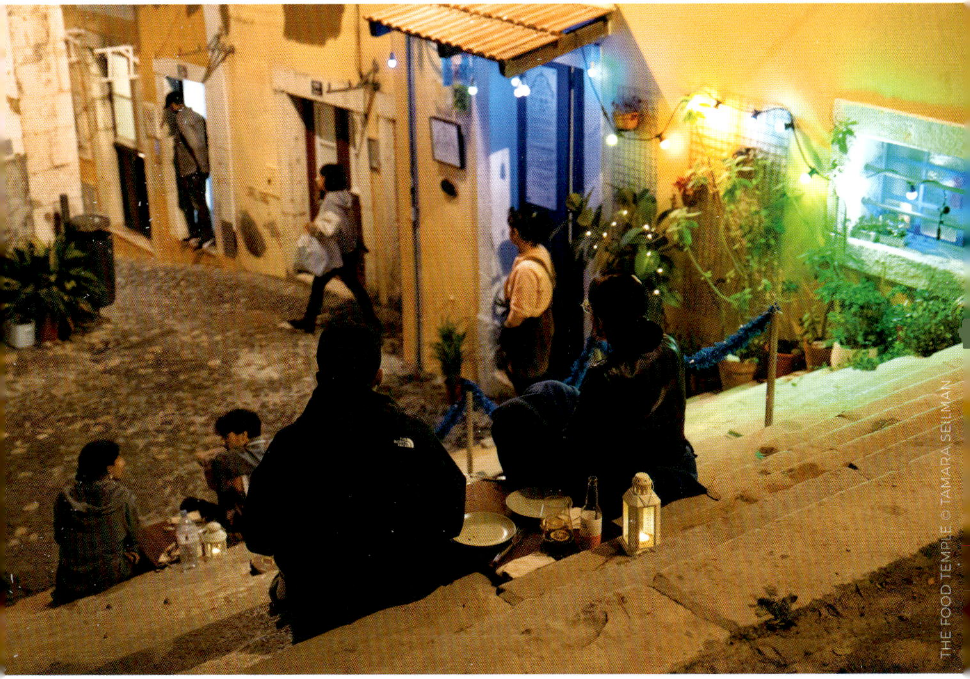
THE FOOD TEMPLE © TAMARA SEILMAN

© LUCIE ETCHEBERS

THE FOOD TEMPLE © MARIA MEDICI

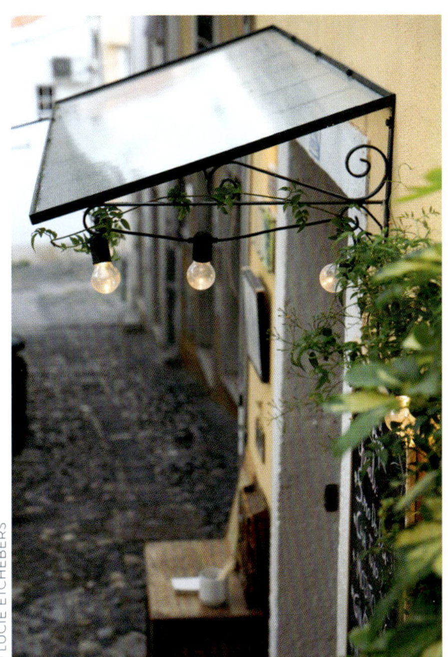

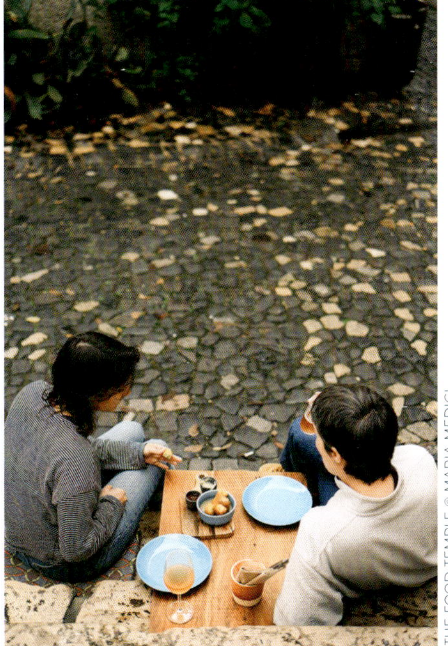

SMALL CAFE,
WIDE ANGLE

Exploring, walking, climbing, running … That's all well and good, but where's the R&R in all this? It's right here, at this cafe under a theatre. Take a little break and settle down in one of the armchairs facing the enormous windows – just long enough to bring your heart rate back down, check in with yourself and drink a latte while taking in the panoramic view of Lisbon.

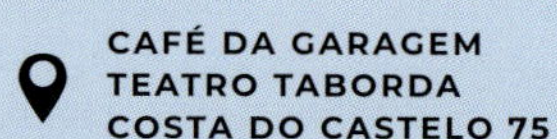

CAFÉ DA GARAGEM
TEATRO TABORDA
COSTA DO CASTELO 75

+351 21 885 4190

Instagram: @cafe.dagaragem
teatrodagaragem.com/en/cafe-da-garagem

CAFÉ DA GARAGEM

SPEND A NIGHT AT
SANTA CLARA 1728

There are places that exist beyond the limits of time, trends and words. The Santa Clara 1728 hotel is one of them. Within the walls of this 18th-century palace, six rooms and a table d'hôte straight out of a minimalist dream are a blend of white, beige, blond wood and authentic period stone. Outside, in the world at large, our attention is constantly being solicited. Here, behind the Santa Clara's large doors and its windows overlooking the National Pantheon, in these rooms in which nothing is super-fluous, silence reigns, the mind grows calm and sets sail, the soul takes flight … Which is one definition of luxury.

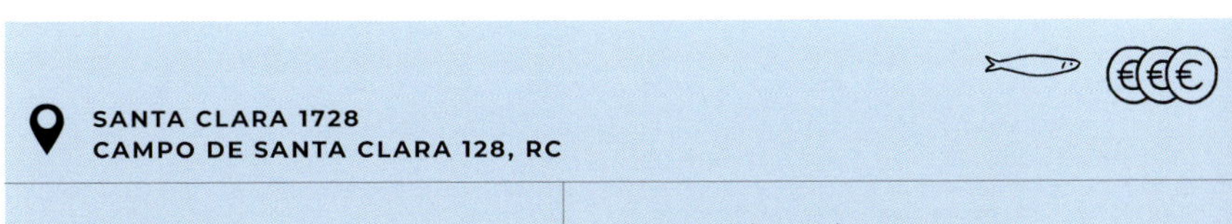

SANTA CLARA 1728
© PIERRE VERDOUX

Designed by the same architectural firm (Atelier Aires Mateus) as Santa Clara 1728 but with a more reasonable budget, Montecarmo 12 is an excellent address.

The pretty rooms, each equipped with an elegant, understated stone bathtub, are arranged around the beautiful spiral staircase that encapsulates the soul of this revamped historic residence in the heart of the Principe Real district.

They serve a delicious breakfast too.

© NELSON GARRIDO

- JOÃO RODRIGUES -

MANAGER OF THE SILENT LIVING GUESTHOUSES

João Rodrigues juggles gracefully. In addition to his career as an airline pilot, he also owns four exceptional guesthouses in Portugal, including Santa Clara 1728 in Lisbon. We met him over a classic breakfast.

What made you want to open guesthouses?
When I was little, my parents' home was always open and filled with people. That inspired me for the future!

What's the story behind Santa Clara 1728?
The first time I saw this building, it was under renovation. I climbed the façade and that's when I fell for the view: the National Pantheon on one side, the convent and monastery of São Vicente de Fora on the other, and, in the far background, the Tagus. I knew I had to live here and open a guesthouse in this old neighborhood tucked between Alfama and Graça.

How would you define the 'Silent Living' philosophy?
It permeates Santa Clara, whose

© PHILIPPA LANGELY

large volumes recall an ancient monastery. It's about respecting traditional architecture and materials, developing a minimalist esthetic around them, and distilling an atmosphere that's reminiscent of a family home ... And, at the heart of this philosophy is the idea that when you enter here, you leave behind the hustle and bustle and demands of the outside world – everything that disturbs peace of mind.

What's your view of Lisbon?

The Tagus embraces the city, opening its arms wide to it. That's what moves me most about this city: its connection to the water. And for me, as someone who is always on the move as part of my profession, Lisbon is the home that welcomes me with open arms every time I return.

Your favorite places?

The Gulbenkian Museum, its gardens, which are the work of Portugal's best landscape designers. I also love Belém, even though it has changed over the years. When I try to go back to a place, I'd like to reconnect with my memories; often it isn't possible because it has closed down or been replaced ...

© NELSON GARRIDO

Is that what's meant by *saudade*?

Yes. It has to do with our history, the age of great discoveries in the 15th and 16th centuries. People left, and you never knew if they would return. That's the origin of this feeling of absence, this nostalgia – a powerful emotion.

One last Lisbon secret?

The best time to enjoy the city is ... in February. The streets are emptier, time is distilled more slowly, and the light is as gorgeous as ever.

UNCOVER THE SECRET
SPOT WHERE FADO
SINGERS HIDE AWAY

First, you find yourself facing a heavy blue wooden door adorned with a gilded handle: magisterial, intimidating. Then you attempt to open it before realising that you have to ring the bell. Someone opens the door for you. It's here, in the dim interior of this 18th-century building decorated with old azulejo tiles, that the city's fado singers meet up after having sung their hearts out elsewhere.

The musicians gradually trickle into their sanctuary. Around 11pm, a fadista sings the saudade accompanied by two guitar players, linking gesture with voice, emotion with the expression in their eyes ... A few minutes later, another voice, other musicians, will take over, but the thrill remains the same: fado. And the performance doesn't let up until sleep finally wins out – sometimes at 2am, sometimes not until breakfast.

MESA DE FRADES
R. DOS REMÉDIOS 139

+351 91 702 9436   mesadefrades.pt   Instagram: @mesadefrades

MESA DE FRADES

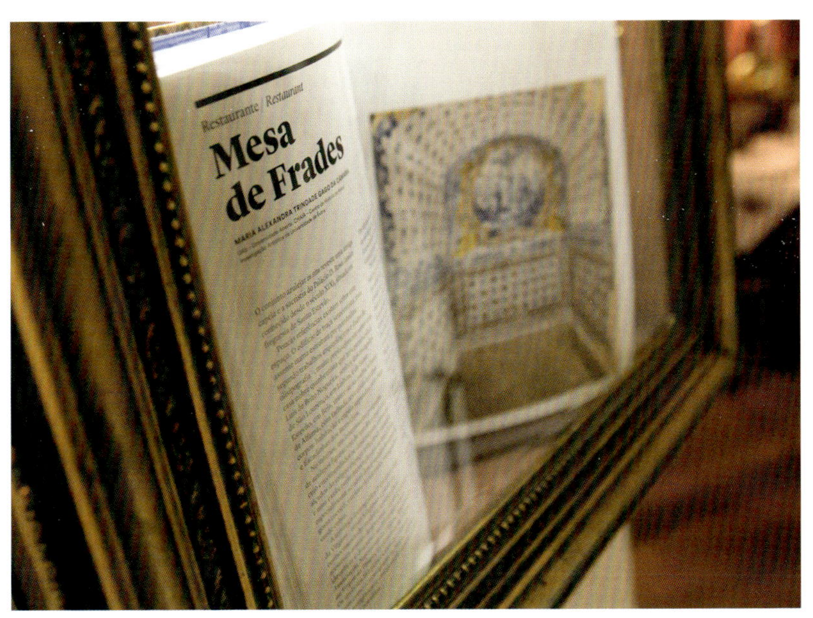
Restaurante / Restaurant
Mesa
de Frades

COLOURFUL
CUISINE

Turning into a narrow alley in Alfama, you'll find Roda Viva, the best Mozambican restaurant in Lisbon. The owner, Chamba, a former *pizzaiolo*, is both friendly and professional. He's been a chef since 2014, using recipes mainly inherited from his grandmother: a clever mix of flavours from Africa, India and Macau. For example, you can gorge on crab and shrimp curries, a delicious chicken with peanuts and some emblematic homely dishes such as *mathapa* (cassava leaf and coconut sauce), Chamba's favourite dish. His secret to success? 'Being happy and in a good mood', undoubtedly the best recipe handed down by his dear grandmother. Don't leave without a pot of homemade spicy sauce.

VAGO
© LUIS GALA

LISA
© @SHOTBYTEJA

MUSIC, COCKTAILS
AND TAPAS

Opened in late 2021 by globetrotting DJs of Colombian, Brazilian, Turkish and Portuguese heritage, Vago is just what Lisbon's nightlife scene was missing. In the early evening, head here to listen to a fantastic music programme (house, techno, samba, zouk, afrobeat ...), have a drink (great cocktails) and eat delicious *petiscos* (Portuguese-style tapas) created by chef Leonor Godinho. Later in the night, come to dance – and more.

Run by the same owners, Lisa is just a few buildings further down on the same street. Every night, it features live DJs and musicians playing jazz, contemporary music, rock, folk, electro and more.

VAGO
RUA DAS GAIVOTAS 11A

Instagram: @vago.lisboa

LISA
RUA DAS GAIVOTAS 5

salalisa.pt
Instagram: @a.sala.lisa

€

GABINETE
LISBON BREAKFAST

A UNIQUE
TEA EMPORIUM

Located in a magnificent former 19th-century shoe shop, the Companhia Portugueza do Chá (Portuguese Tea Company) is a small gem: the moment you open the door, you're enveloped by the powerful scent of this leaf, which, according to the 5th- or 6th-century Chinese Buddhist monk Bodhidharma, promotes concentration and meditation.

Ensconced on lacquered shelves, the elegant tins hold 250 blends of tea: varieties from the most prized plantations in India, Nepal, Sri Lanka (Ceylon), China, Japan, Taiwan, Vietnam and Korea, as well as from Latin America, Africa and the Azores …

The blends, flavoured with organic fruit or flowers, are created by the Argentinian owner, Sebastian Filgueiras. In his workshop at the back, Sebastian also regularly dreams up new flavours: Japanese yuzu and green tea, black tea with grapefruit, and fruit infusions that are perfect for enjoying iced.

- SEBASTIAN FILGUEIRAS -

FOUNDER OF COMPANHIA PORTUGUEZA DO CHÁ

Where did you get the idea for this tea emporium?

In Lisbon, small shops that combined the coffee and tea trades had become obsolete, and I wanted to revive this tradition by expanding the range of varieties available and constantly raising the quality. Catherine of Braganza (1638–1705), who made tea fashionable in Europe, has pride of place here: it's her profile that is featured on our tea tins. In the 18th century, every garden in the city had tea pavilions, a legacy of the strong ties between Portugal and the East.

What's your favourite tea?

The loose-leaf tea of my childhood – usually black tea from China, Assam or

Ceylon. Strong teas.
In northern Portugal,
where my wife grew up,
serving black tea to
children before school –
and in hospital too – was
also very common. Very
often it was tea from
Mozambique or Ceylon.
Tea bags didn't come
along until much later.

What inspires your blends?
The light of this city, the
culture of this country, its
literature, its history …
I started with Lisbon
Breakfast, a blend of Ceylon
tea and black tea grown in
the Azores. It's bright and
well-balanced, a good
everyday morning tea.
Our Earl Grey Portugal is
flavoured with the peel of
bergamot grown on a farm
in the Alentejo region:
we dry it ourselves. Many
of our teas are exclusive.

**What's the rarest tea
available here?**
Thousand-Year Tea. It's
grown in the Yunnan
region of China, and what
makes it unique is that its
leaves are picked from a
single tree, probably one of
the oldest in the world.
It's even listed as one of
China's heritage tea trees.
The taste is impossible to
define – it's mild yet
powerful. I put myself on a
waiting list for this tea every
year … and never receive
more than 2 kg.

BAR, BOOKSTORE, CINEMA, CONCERTS, DJ SETS ...
AN ESSENTIAL VENUE

It was the cultural venue that was missing in Lisbon and a long-time dream of owner José Pinho, founder of bookstore Ler Devagar in the LX Factory west of central Lisbon.

In the middle of Bairro Alto, this former outbuilding of a three-storey convent is a refuge for locals. They gather here at the end of their busy days to have a drink, a bite to eat or simply take a break.

The building also has a bookstore, film screenings, exhibitions, live concerts and DJ sets.

In a very relaxed atmosphere, the bar serves some mouthwatering snacks including a 'pulled pork' mushroom sandwich to die for and much else. All this can be enjoyed in the Museu da Preguiça (Museum of Laziness), a room with beds. A rest before finally joining the dance floor.

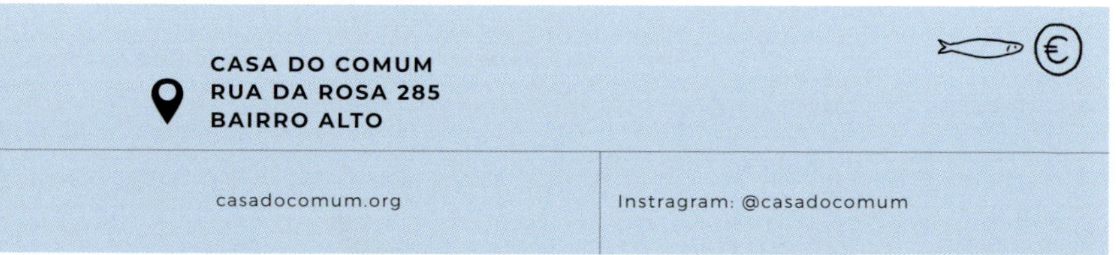

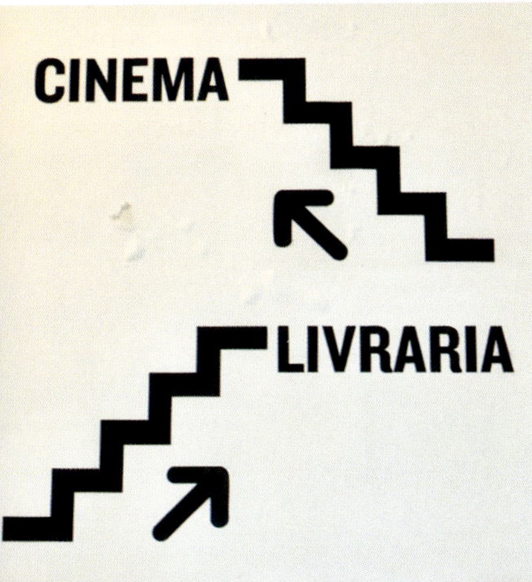
CINEMA
LIVRARIA
BAR

SOAK UP THE ATMOSPHERE
OF PRAÇA DAS FLORES

In Lisbon, all roads lead to the charming Praça das Flores, a small shady square in the heart of the Príncipe Real district. Its fountain, lavender-blue kiosk and wooden benches make it look like a cinema decor. However, what draws visitors there most often are the multitude of bars, restaurants and shops scattered about the area. During the day the atmosphere is peaceful. You can daydream with a coffee accompanied by the famous Portuguese egg custard tart known as *pastel de nata*. However, as soon as the sun goes down, 'Flower Square' comes alive. People meet there to have a drink, something to eat or just enjoy the sweet evenings in Lisbon.

In the square itself, at **Magnolia**, you sit on the terrace (or at the only indoor table near the open window overlooking the square) to share some tapas and a good glass of wine. The signature dish of the restaurant: oven-cooked Camembert sprinkled with honey.

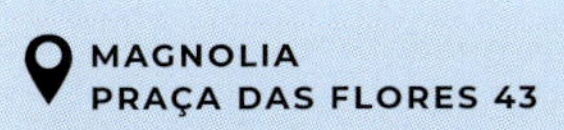

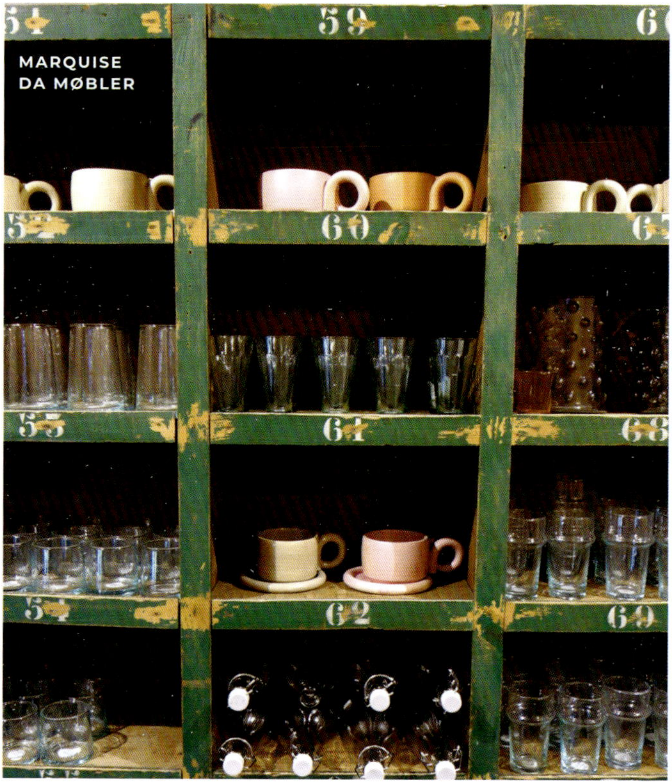

© LUCIE ETCHEBERS

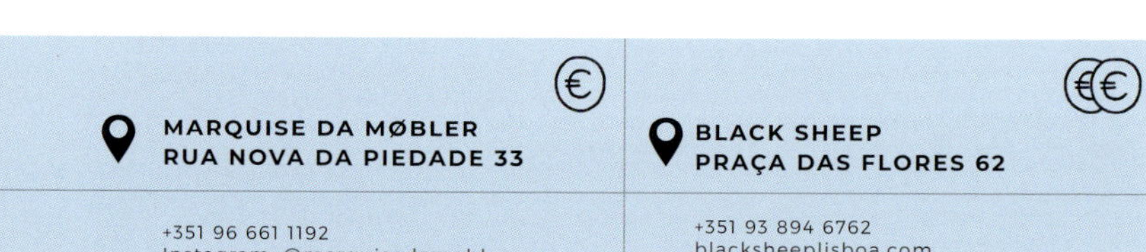

Close to the square, **Marquise da Møbler** is the most charming tea room / concept store in Príncipe Real. All the objects you'll see around are for sale. Its little secret is the interior patio hidden from the street. Perfect for breakfast or brunch.

In front of the kiosk, the **Black Sheep** offers one of the best selections of wines in Lisbon. From time to time the owner and chief wine waiter Lucas Ferreira takes out his guitar to accompany the tranquility that reigns on the square.

€

MARQUISE DA MØBLER
RUA NOVA DA PIEDADE 33

+351 96 661 1192
Instagram: @marquisedamobler

€€

BLACK SHEEP
PRAÇA DAS FLORES 62

+351 93 894 6762
blacksheeplisboa.com
Instagram: @blacksheeplisboa

MARQUISE DA MØBLER
© LUCIE ETCHEBERS

THE BEST-EVER
VEGETARIAN
RESTAURANT

Created in 2019 by João Ricardo Alves, a Portuguese-Brazilian chef, and Alejandro Chávarro, a naturalised French Colombian, Arkhe is an exceptional experience. It's very likely the best vegetarian restaurant you've ever tried – and at perfectly acceptable prices, considering the quality of the food.

A great deal of thought, passion and incredible talent goes into everything at Arkhe. And you can look forward to a warm and impeccably professional welcome from Alejandro, who used to manage Michelin-starred restaurants in France and Spain and is also a top-class sommelier.

An absolute must.

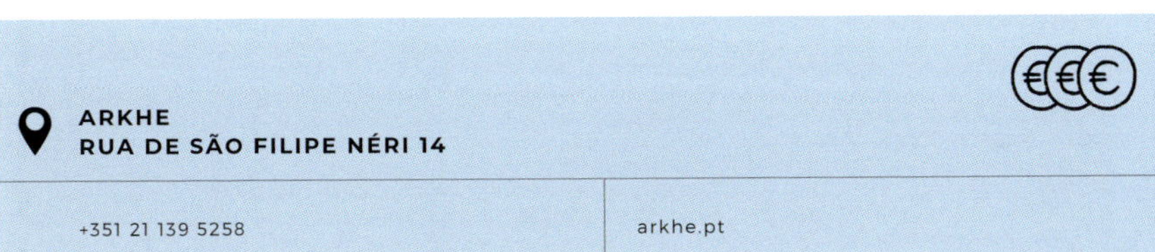

TALK TO STRANGERS
AT PROCÓPIO

Since 1972, the little red door to this nightclub has seen many insiders pass through, here to lose all sense of time. In fact, in the small room, where waiters flit about in bow ties, styles and centuries seem to collapse in on themselves: tasselled lampshades brush against armchairs, knick-knacks flirt with illustrations from the 1930s ... To make sure you don't miss a thing, choose the table at the back perched on a small platform or a seat at the bar, while sipping a Caipï or Amendoa Amarga.

NB: Since we're still sort of stuck in 1972 here, smoking is permitted.

PASTÉIS DE NATA VS ELEPHANT EARS: SHOWDOWN OF THE SWEETS

PASTÉIS DE NATA

If Lisbon had a flavour, it would be the *pastel de nata* (custard tart) – never mind that this pastry was actually invented in the 19th century by nuns in the convent in Belém (which was still separate from Lisbon at the time). Since 1837, the Pastelaria de Belém has been carrying on this tradition, selling these *pastel de Belém* pastries to the hordes of tourists who come here to taste the original – the one that started it all. But you can also avoid a long wait: at the Aloma pastry shop and tea salon, which has won the prize for best *pastel de nata* more than once, the custard tarts are prepared on the spot, served lukewarm, dusted with cinnamon ... and polished off at the counter in less time than it took to write this sentence. For the most patient among you, treat yourself to the pastel de nata at the superb Jardim da Estrela, located close by.

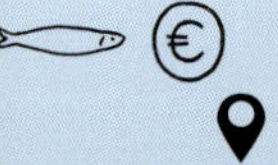

PASTELARIA ALOMA
R. FRANCISCO METRASS 67

Instagram: @pastelaria_aloma
aloma.pt

PASTELARIA O CARECA
R. DUARTE PACHECO PEREIRA 11D

+351 21 301 0987
pastelariaocareca.pt
Instagram: @pastelariacareca

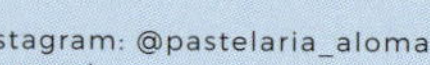

ELEPHANT EARS

Above Belém, in the Restelo neighbourhood, the Pastelaria O Careca is a local institution. Regulars throng to what they call 'the Bald Guy' – the nickname given to the man who originally opened the place in 1954. The price of success? You now have to take a number at the door and wait a few minutes for your turn – just long enough to peruse the amazing display case before choosing the house speciality: elephant-ear cookies. But not just any old elephant ears, the best in town: the perfect balance of flaky, toasted, lightly caramelized, crunchy and sweet.

22

THE LISBON BISTRO
PAR EXCELLENCE

A little way from the touristy areas (which is a relief!), in the pleasant Campo de Ourique district, yet barely a 15-minutes' walk from Principe Real, Bichomau is our kind of bistro: 100% Lisbon, with its pretty blue ceramic decor, excellent food (a new take on Portuguese cuisine) at reasonable prices and a charming atmosphere ... What more could you want?

One of our favourite places in Lisbon.

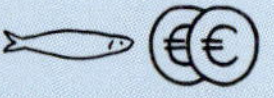

 **BISTRÔ BICHOMAU**
R. COELHO DA ROCHA 21A

+351 21 160 8694

reservation.umai.io/en/widget/bistro-bicho-mau

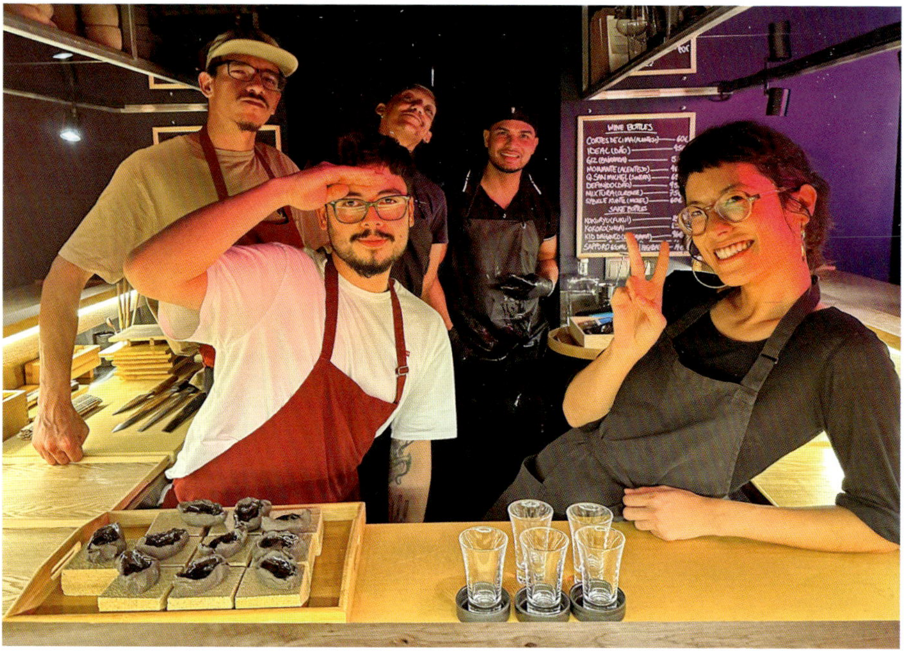
WINE BOTLES
IDEAL (DÃO)
SAKE BOTLES

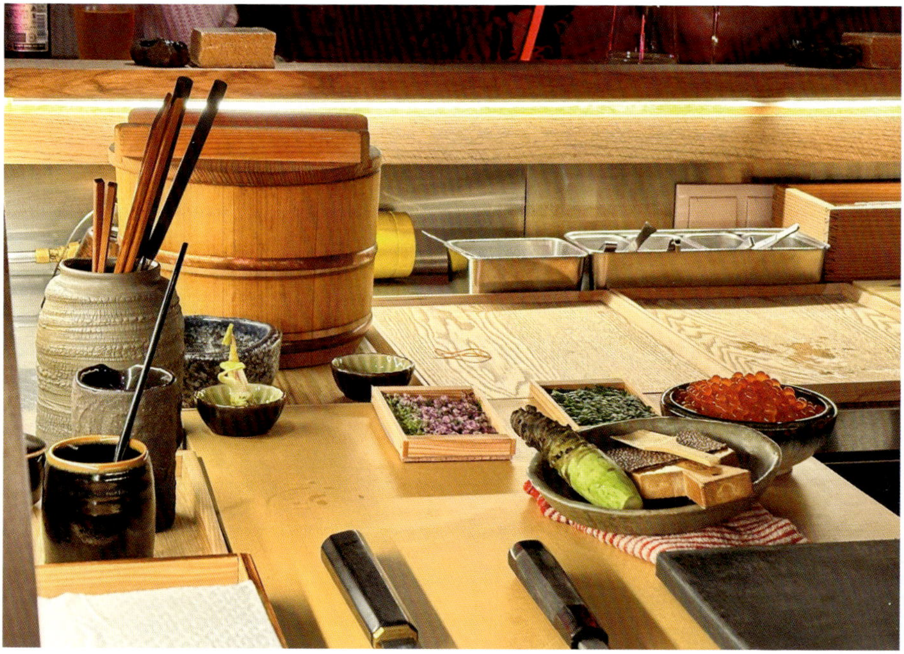

A MASTERPIECE OF A JAPANESE RESTAURANT

With only ten seats around a 'U' counter, Omakase Ri is an exceptional Japanese restaurant where you feel almost privileged to have found a place.

No menu is available (you just tell the very friendly team serving you of any food intolerances). After that, for the next two hours (which pass quickly) you're treated to a parade of dishes whose finesse, refinement and precision are spectacular. As Japanese tradition demands, everything is also beautifully presented and the products used are the freshest they could be. For example, wasabi comes not in a tube but fresh, as in the best restaurants in Japan. Not to be missed.

OMAKASE RI
RUA GARCIA DE ORTA 71C
SHOPPING LAPA 71 STORE 1

+351 91 409 4506
omakaseri.com
Instagram: @omakase.ri

Strongly advised to book well in advance or count on a bit of luck for last-minute places

© CECILE LOPES PHOTOGRAPHY

HAVE A DRINK IN
AN ABANDONED FACTORY

Nestled in the heart of an abandoned factory in the centre of the Alcantara district, Mīrārī is a multipurpose destination that is still relatively unknown.

From Thursday to Monday, this large open-air space at the end of a cul-de-sac hosts concerts, pop-up markets, boules competitions, exhibitions and a range of street-food options (pizza, burgers, poke bowls, artisanal ice creams, etc). On the back wall, a beautiful mural by Franco-Congolese artist Kouka Ntadi Assis completes the decor.

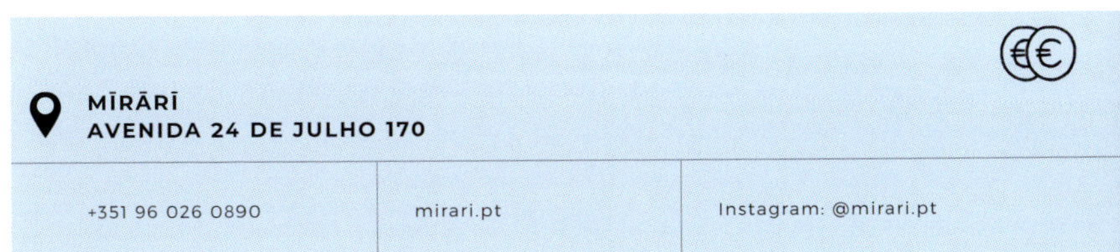

MĪRĀRĪ
AVENIDA 24 DE JULHO 170

+351 96 026 0890   mirari.pt   Instagram: @mirari.pt

RESTAURANTE PONTO FINAL

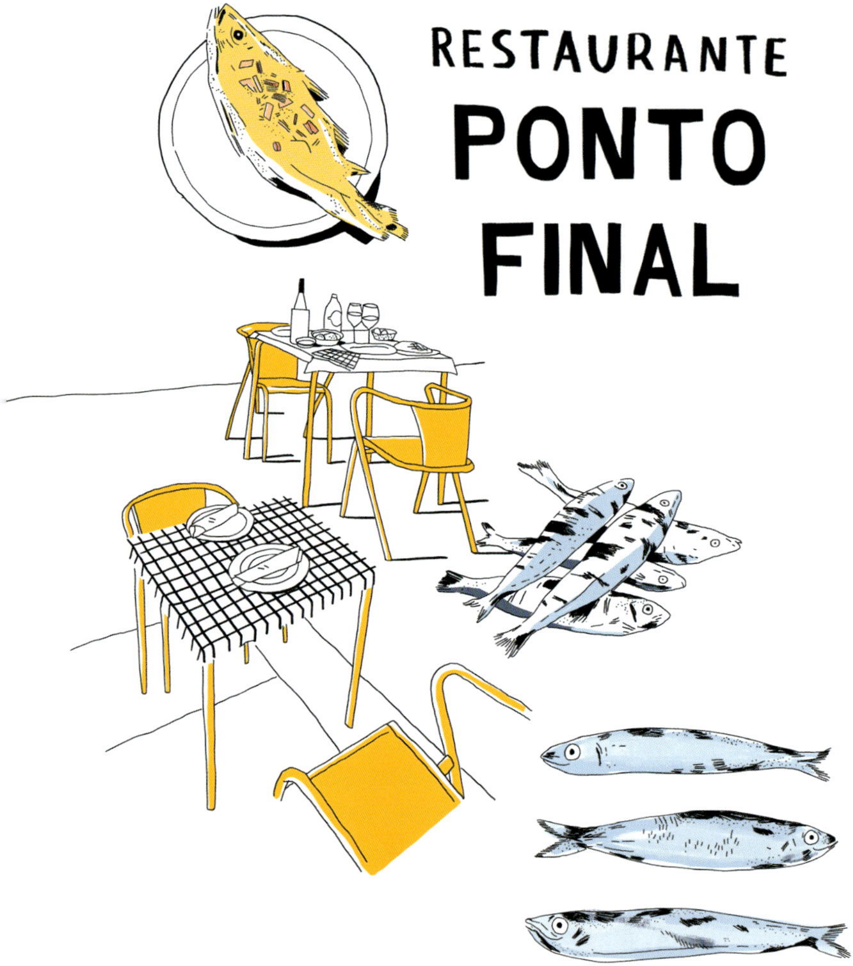

GRILLED FISH
AT PONTO FINAL

A short boat ride and 15 minutes later you're in Cacilhas, on the other side of the Tagus. Grab the table at the very end of the pier, directly across from Lisbon. Murmuring water, the light of the final hours of the day, the simplicity of grilled fish with just a twist of lemon ... If this isn't happiness, it sure comes close.

RESTAURANTE
PONTO
FINAL

PONTO FINAL
© MALLORY BROOKS (BLOGGER)

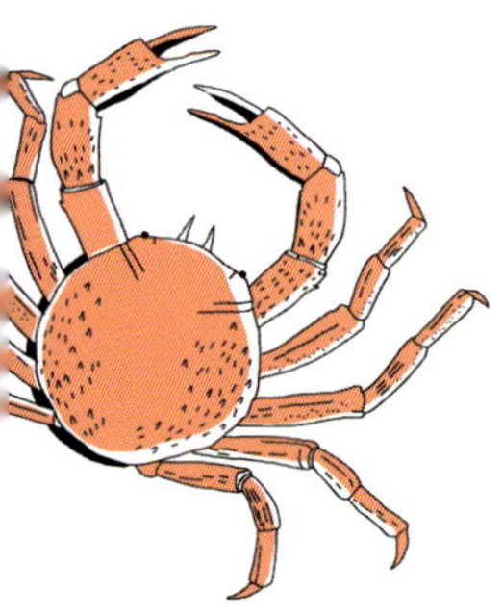

DO YOU DARE TO EAT
A SPIDER CRAB?

A little heads up if you want to try spider crab prepared Lisbon style: get ready to abandon all dignity. The spindly creature is presented to you before it is cooked. When the finished crab arrives, the show begins. Armed with a hammer, you break the shell to excavate the meat, dip it into a delicious sauce made of mayonnaise, mustard, egg, parsley, soft bread, pickles and a pinch of chilli pepper, and then spread the whole thing onto a slice of toast slathered with butter. A culinary delight that's not without its risks: you might very well end up with a bit of crab in your hair or on your shirt. Don't say we didn't warn you. If patience isn't your forte, choose one of these other *marisqueiras* (seafood restaurants), which take reservations : Nune's Real Marisqueira or O Relento.

€€€

CERVEJARIA RAMIRO
AVENIDA ALMIRANTE REIS 1 – H

+351 96 983 9472
cervejariaramiro.com

NUNE'S REAL MARISQUEIRA
R. BARTOLOMEU DIAS

+351 21 301 9899
nunesmarisqueira.pt

O RELENTO
AV. COMBATENTES DA GRANDE GUERRA 10C OEIRAS

+351 21 411 4063

EXPERIENCE
A SURREAL EVENING

About 15 minutes east of central Lisbon by taxi, in the Beato district, the Palacio do Grilo (Palace of the Cricket), which was classified as a monument of public interest in 2011, is a magnificent 18th-century palace. A few years ago, it was transformed into a spectacular restaurant-cum-nightclub with a deliberately surreal atmosphere.

During dinner, which is served in the palace's magnificent main rooms, expect improbable artistic performances amidst the tables. The food is decent – but that's not why you're here.

After dinner, at weekends, head for the nightclub, where the DJs and bar staff, donning costumes and sometimes masks, set the tone for a decidedly offbeat evening.

One-of-a-kind in Lisbon.

 **PALACIO DO GRILO – GALA CRICRI**
CALÇADA DO DUQUE DE LAFÕES 1

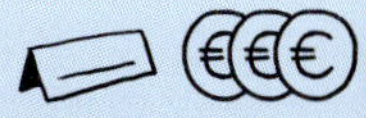

+351 91 044 0942 | palaciogrilo.com galacricri.com | Instagram: @palaciodogrilo and @galacricri

A BERLIN CLUB
IN LISBON

Rumours spread across the city like wildfire in 2023 when Outra Cena opened in a disused former winery in Marvila. Success was immediate, maybe because there was no other place like it in Lisbon, and there still isn't.

In this huge concrete cathedral, the atmosphere is industrial and, as in the founding nightclub in Berlin (Berghain), phones are banned. This lets you stop filming and taking photos, instead giving you the rare opportunity to live in the moment, to let go completely and dance like there's no tomorrow. And it feels good …

The club frequently attracts big names from the electronic scene.

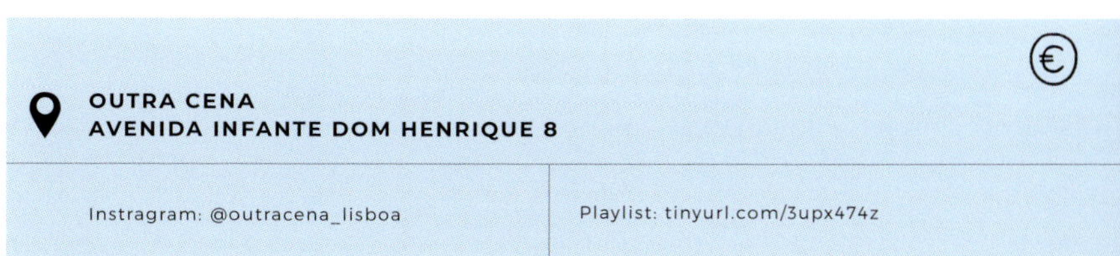

DISCOVERING
THE EAST OF THE CITY

In Marvila, to the east of the city, a neighbourhood that's constantly moving up and up, 8 Marvila is a sprawling 22,000-square-metre warehouse conversion. It was originally built in 1917 to store as much as 5 million litres of Pereira da Fonseca wine in vast vats that now house the new venues.

The cultural and commercial space offers everything from an eclectic interior design store to vegetarian doughnuts, Mexican and Japanese restaurants alongside vintage clothes, vinyl records, a pizzeria, an upscale garden centre called Planta Livre, astrology, reiki and massage therapies. There's also eight paddle tennis courts and even an indoor Pickleball court.

8 MARVILA
PRAÇA DAVID LEANDRO DA SILVA 8

8marvila.com

Instagram: @8marvila

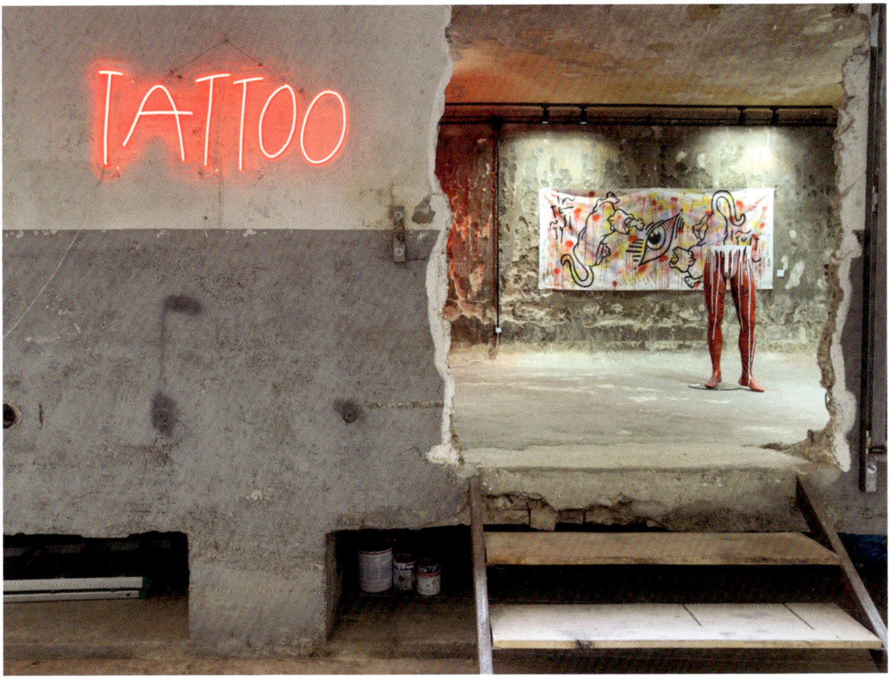

TATTOO

ABEL PEREIRA DA FONSECA
ABEL PEREIRA DA FONSECA

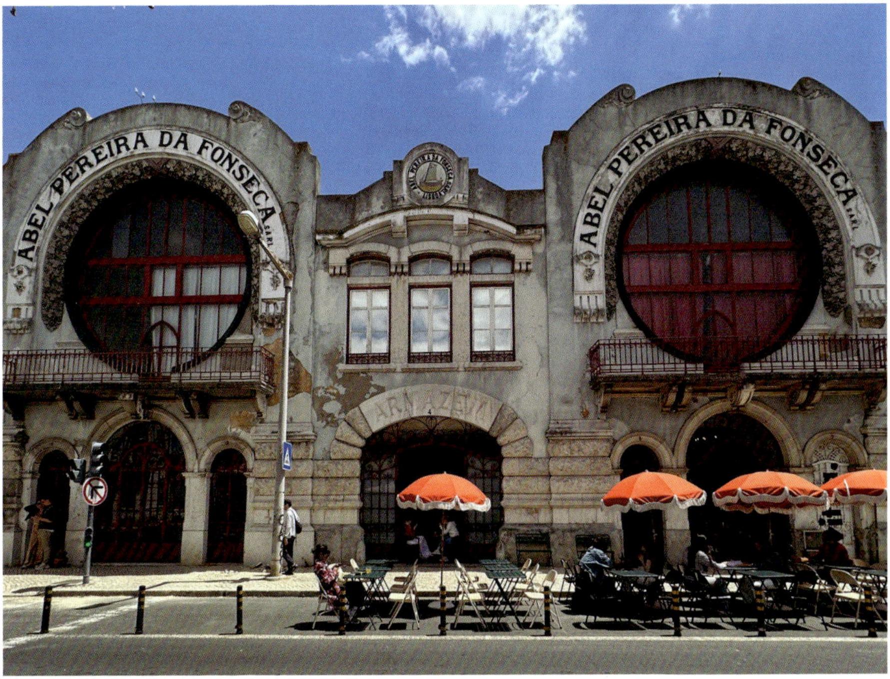

CENTRO
RESTA
ES PU
EXC
M
@

Go check it out quickly as the privately owned space is destined for a mega luxury real-estate project.

Don't miss the Night Market until midnight on Saturdays, or the organic brunches at Dear Breakfast alongside restaurant and bar MATO's vegetarian pizzas.

The Outra Cena club (see p. 111) is literally glued to 8 Marvila and the wonderful Fábrica Braço de Prata (Silver Arms Factory, p. 119) is a 3-minute walk away ...

SAÍDA
SAÍDA

AN ALTERNATIVE
NIGHT OUT
IN MARVILA

Nights out in the east of Lisbon, between Marvila's industrial relics and the cultural revival, have never been so lively.

Housed in a long-abandoned former ammunitions factory, hence its name ('Silver Arms Factory'), the Fábrica Braço de Prata has been the city's most interesting alternative location since 2007.

This immense space (twelve rooms) where restaurant, concerts, exhibitions, literary meetings, plays, dance classes and raves are interwoven, is constantly reinventing itself. Explore and be inspired.

 **FÁBRICA BRAÇO DE PRATA**
RUA DA FÁBRICA DO MATERIAL DE GUERRA 1
MARVILA

fabricabracodeprata.com

Instagram: @fabricabracodeprata

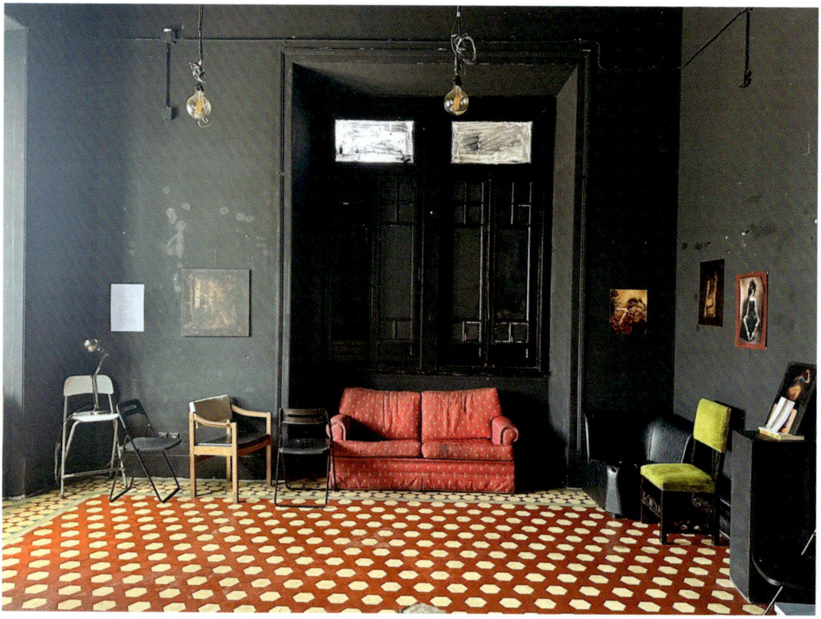

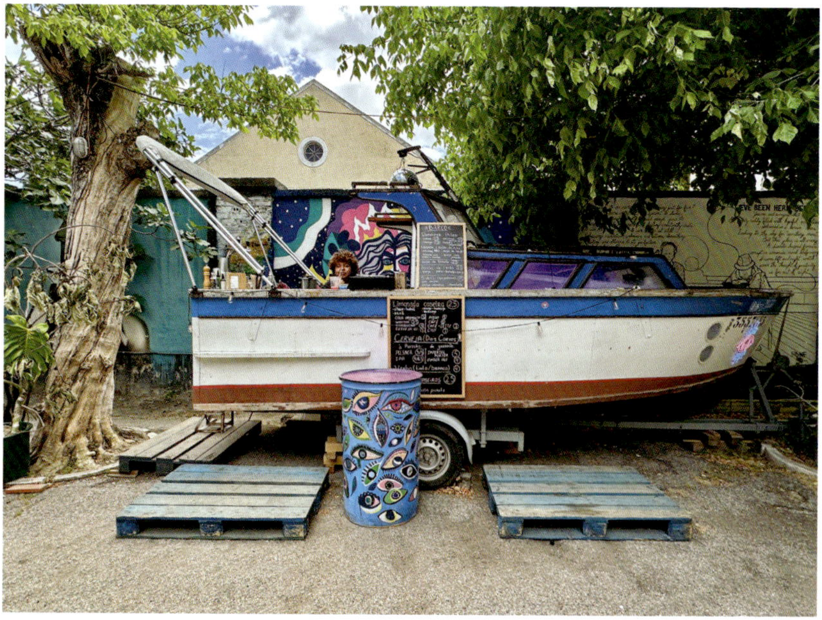
Limonada caseira 2,5
CERVEJA (Dois Corvos)

THE SECRET CHINESE RESTAURANT
YOU NEEDED, OF COURSE

In Mouraria district, look for the blue door in Rua Marquês Ponte de Lima.

Press the red button on the intercom.

Show your credentials and go up a floor.

Order the dumplings.

You're welcome.

**SECRET
ADDRESS**

34
quot

MUITO OBRIGADO / MANY THANKS TO

Jérôme C, João-Maria MS, Sofia M, Peter O, Chloé S, Miguel C, Miguel J, Alexander W, Nelson P, Rita A, Luca P, Ruben O and Anne-Laure B

This book was created by:
Fany Péchiodat, Lauriane Gepner and Lucie Etchebers, authors
Nathalie Chebou, project manager
Coline Girard, illustrator
Paula Franco @lisbonbylight, photographer
Emmanuelle Willard Toulemonde, layout
Sophie Schlondorff and Sonny Alexander, translation
Jana Gough and Caroline Lawrence, editing
Kimberly Bess, proofreading
Mado De La Quintinie, publishing

Cover photo: © Beth Chobanova – Unsplash

You can write to us at info@editionsjonglez.com
Follow us on Instagram: @editionsjonglez

THANKS

From the same publisher

Photo Books

Abandoned America: The Age of Consequences
Abandoned Asylums
Abandoned Australia
Abandoned Belgium
Abandoned Churches: Unclaimed Places of Worship
Abandoned Cinemas of the World
Abandoned France
Abandoned Germany
Abandoned Lebanon
Abandoned Italy
Abandoned Japan
Abandoned Spain
Abandoned USSR
Abandoned World - An AI-generated exploration
After the Final Curtain: The Fall of the American Movie Theater
After the Final Curtain: America's Abandoned Theaters
Baikonur - Vestiges of the Soviet Space Program
Cinemas - A French Heritage
Chernobyl's Atomic Legacy - 25 years after disaster
Clickbait - A visual journey through AI-generated stories
Destination: Wellness - Our 35 best places in the world to make a pause
Forbidden Places - Exploring our Abandoned Heritage
Forbidden France
Forgotten Heritage
Private Islands for Rent
Oblivion
Secret Sacred Sites
Unusual Hotels Europe
Unusual Hotels - World
Unusual Hotels UK & Ireland
Unusual Nights in Paris
Unusual Shopping in Paris
Unusual Wines
Venice deserted

'Soul of' Guides

Soul of Amsterdam - A guide to the 30 best experiences
Soul of Athens - A guide to 30 exceptional experiences
Soul of Barcelona - 30 experiences
Soul of Berlin - A guide to the 30 best experiences
Soul of Brussels - A guide to exceptional experiences
Soul of Detroit - A guide to exceptional experiences
Soul of Kyoto - A guide to exceptional experiences
Soul of Los Angeles - A guide to 30 exceptional experiences
Soul of Marrakesh - A guide to 30 exceptional experiences
Soul of Marseille - A guide to exceptional experiences
Soul of Milan - A guide to exceptional experiences
Soul of New York - A guide to 30 exceptional experiences
Soul of Paris - 30 experiences
Soul of Rome - A guide to exceptional experiences
Soul of Tokyo - A guide to exceptional experiences
Soul of Venice - A guide to 30 exceptional experiences

Atlas

Atlas of forbidden places
Atlas of geographical curiosities
Atlas of extreme weather
Atlas of unusual wines

'Secret' Guides

Secret Amsterdam
Secret Bali - An unusual guide
Secret Bangkok
Secret Barcelona
Secret Bars & Restaurants in Paris
Secret Bath - An unusual guide
Secret Belfast
Secret Berlin
Secret Boston - An unusual guide
Secret Brighton - An unusual guide
Secret Brooklyn
Secret Brussels
Secret Budapest
Secret Buenos Aires
Secret Campania
Secret Cape Town
Secret Copenhagen
Secret Corsica
Secret Dolomites
Secret Dublin - An unusual guide
Secret Edinburgh - An unusual guide
Secret Florence
Secret French Riviera
Secret Geneva
Secret Glasgow
Secret Granada
Secret Helsinki
Secret Istanbul
Secret Johannesburg
Secret Lisbon

Secret Liverpool - An unusual guide
Secret London - An unusual guide
Secret London - Unusual Bars & Restaurants
Secret Los Angeles - An unusual guide
Secret Louisiana
Secret Madrid
Secret Mexico City
Secret Milan
Secret Montreal - An unusual guide
Secret Naples
Secret New Orleans - An unusual guide
Secret New York - An unusual guide
Secret New York - Curious Activities
Secret New York - Hidden Bars & Restaurants
Secret Normandy
Secret Paris
Secret Postdam
Secret Prague
Secret Provence
Secret Rio
Secret Rome
Secret Seville
Secret Singapore
Secret Stockholm
Secret Sussex - An unusual guide
Secret Tokyo
Secret Tuscany
Secret Venice
Secret Vienna
Secret Washington DC - An unusual guide

Follow us on Facebook and Instagram

© JONGLEZ 2025
Registration of copyright: June 2025 – Edition : 03
ISBN: 978-2-36195-926-5
Printed in Slovakia by Polygraf